OHIO
DOMINICAN
UNIVERSITY™

SINCE 1911

OHIO DOMINICAN UNIVERSITY

1216 SUNBURY ROAD

COLUMBUS, OHIO 43219-2099

WAR AND THE PITY OF WAR

WAR AND THE PITY OF WAR

EDITED BY NEIL PHILIP

ILLUSTRATED BY MICHAEL McCURDY

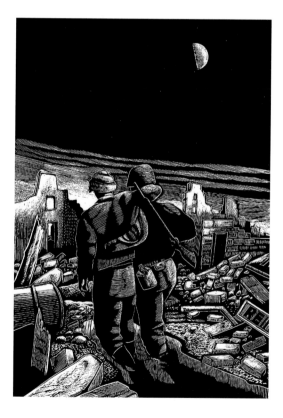

CLARION BOOKS
New York

IN MEMORY OF MY FATHER
JOHN MATTHEW CHISHOLM PHILIP

Clarion Books
A Houghton Mifflin Company imprint
215 Park Avenue South, New York, NY 10003

Published in The United States in 1998 by arrangement with
The Albion Press Ltd, Spring Hill, Idbury, Oxfordshire OX7 6RU, England

Volume copyright © 1998 The Albion Press Ltd
Illustrations copyright © 1998 Michael McCurdy
Selection and introduction copyright © 1998 Neil Philip
Copyright in individual passages copyright © 1998 as noted specifically in
the acknowledgments on p. 96

For information about permission to reproduce selections from this book
write to Permissions, Houghton Mifflin Company, 215 Park Avenue South,
New York, NY 10003

Library of Congress Cataloging-in-Publication Data

War and the pity of war / edited by Neil Philip; illustrated by
Michael McCurdy.
p. cm.
Includes indexes.
Summary: Presents an illustrated collection of poems about the
waste, horror, and futility of war as well as the nobility, courage,
and sacrifice of individuals in wartime.
ISBN 0-395-84982-9
1. War—Juvenile poetry. 2. Children's poetry. [1. War—Poetry.
2. Poetry—Collections.] I. Philip. Neil. II. McCurdy, Michael. ill.
PN6110.W28W37   1998
808.81'9358—dc21   97-32897
                                                          CIP
                                                          AC

Permissions: Connie Hallam
Design: Emma Bradford

Typesetting by York House Typographic, London
Printed in Hong Kong

10 9 8 7 6 5 4 3 2 1

CONTENTS

INTRODUCTION

The seventeenth-century cavalier poet Sir Richard Lovelace wrote a pretty lyric entitled "To Lucasta, Going to the Wars." Its last lines are deservedly famous:

> I could not love thee, dear, so much,
> Loved I not honour more.

This attitude—that war was the natural mode of expression for the manly virtues—can be traced right back to the beginnings of poetry, and right forward to the early years of the present century. In the personal columns of the London *Times* in 1914, two days before the First World War was declared, someone posted the notice: "PAULINE—Alas, it cannot be. But I will dash into the great venture with all that pride and spirit an ancient race has given me...."

This was the attitude with which poets entered the field in 1914. But in the crucible of terror that was the so-called Great War, a new kind of war poetry was forged. Dreams of honor and glory died an agonizing death on the killing fields of the Western Front. This was the world's first experience of total war—a glimpse into the abyss. At the battle of the Somme in 1916 over a million men died—a mass slaughter unparalleled in history. The war poet Edmund Blunden recalled his feelings after the desperate opening round of battle: "By the end of the day both sides had seen, in a sad scrawl of broken earth and murdered men, the answer to the question. No road. No thoroughfare. Neither race had won, nor could win, the War. The War had won, and would go on winning."

From this experience of horror and degradation, a new type of war poet emerged. Writers such as Blunden, Siegfried Sassoon, and Ivor Gurney wanted not to celebrate war but to express the disgust they felt at its futility—the absurdity and pointlessness of it, the sense that "The War had won, and would go on winning."

One such First World War poet, Wilfred Owen, wrote in a Preface to his war poems:

> My subject is War, and the pity of War.
> The poetry is in the pity.

Owen explicitly refused as possible themes "anything about glory, honour, might, majesty, dominion, or power."

These words provide the keynote to most war poetry that has been written since—certainly in the English language. Politicians may still present war in terms of honor and glory; poets and, notably in Vietnam, journalists, speak of pity and waste.

For Owen, then, and for most modern poets, war is about horror, not heroism. Yet Owen himself was a war hero. In October 1918 he won the Military Cross for an act of personal bravery; a month later, in the last days of a senseless war which laid waste a generation of poets, he was killed in action. He had described himself in a letter as "a conscientious objector with a very seared conscience."

The First World War brought about a shift in sensibility in both poets and readers. It is the cruelty of war, not its glory, which is at the forefront of our minds. And because of this we may read the war poetry of earlier generations with different eyes. For instance the earliest surviving Welsh poem is Aneirin's "Y Gododdin," an heroic account, dating from about 600 A.D., of a war raid in which the entire three-hundred-strong war party of the Gododdin is overpowered and slaughtered. The poem, an elegy for the warriors, celebrates their brave deaths. In the translation of A. O. H. Jarman, one passage reads:

> Three hundred gold-torqued warriors,
> Warlike, splendid in action,
> Three hundred haughty ones,
> Of one mind, fully armed;
> Three hundred impetuous horses
> Charged forward with them,
> Three hounds and three hundred,
> Alas, they did not return.

To readers today, the loss of these three hundred seems more tragic than heroic—as pointless as the deaths of the six hundred in Alfred, Lord Tennyson's "Charge of the Light Brigade," or the trench soldiers left "hanging on the old barbed wire" in the First World War song.

For while earlier poetry did celebrate war and warriors, it also counted the cost. The first words of Virgil's *Aeneid* are *Arma virumque cano*—"I sing of arms and the man." But amid the glory and excitement, there is room too for the pain of Owen's "seared conscience." Virgil's Aeneas, recounting the destruction of Troy, says, "No man could speak of such things and not weep."

In a similar way, twentieth-century war poets, while rejecting the idea of war as a game in which the prize is honor and glory, record the bravery, dignity, and humanity of those caught up in war's horrors—both soldiers and civilians.

One of the things which I hope this collection will show is how similar the experience of both war and soldiering has been throughout human history. War has always seemed "total warfare" to those in the thick of the fighting. Battle has always been both elating and numbing. Soldiers have always felt bored, homesick, and frightened.

Bunno's "Pick a fern, pick a fern," from the eleventh century B.C., finds echoes in W. H. Auden's vividly imagined "Roman Wall Blues" and in the tense unreality of the "Jungle Night" in a poem by "K," an anonymous British soldier in Burma in the 1940s. Rudyard Kipling's "Epitaphs of the War, 1914–18" share the economy and power of epitaphs from *The Greek Anthology* by writers such as Anakreon and Simonides from the sixth and fifth centuries B.C. "Central Highlands, Viet Nam, 1968," by the Cherokee/Quapaw/Chickasaw poet Geary Hobson, is recognizably in the same tradition as Henry Rowe Schoolcraft's early nineteenth-century version of Ojibwa "War Songs."

There are poems here from Beirut and Bosnia, and from ancient China and ancient Greece. If the book is dominated by the great conflicts of this century, I hope nevertheless that there is enough from earlier days to set our century's story in the wider context of human history and human suffering.

Israeli poet Dan Pagis, in his poem "Written in Pencil in the Sealed Railway-Car," links the terrors of the Holocaust to the first murder, when Cain slew his brother Abel; Carl Sandburg, in "Wars," envisaged "In the wars to come new silent deaths, new silent hurlers not yet dreamed out in the heads of men."

Poetry may seem an irrelevance in the face of tragedies such as the Holocaust or the destruction of Hiroshima by an atomic bomb. But it is finally only through poetry that we can understand their meaning. That is why, as Owen also wrote, "the true Poets must be truthful."

Neil Philip

WAR POET

Sidney Keyes

Second World War

I am the man who looked for peace and found
My own eyes barbed.
I am the man who groped for words and found
An arrow in my hand.
I am the builder whose firm walls surround
A slipping land.
When I grow sick or mad
Mock me not nor chain me:
When I reach for the wind
Cast me not down:
Though my face is a burnt book
And a wasted town.

PAPER SOLDIER

Bulat Okudzhava

1959

TRANSLATED FROM THE RUSSIAN BY ALBERT C. TODD

There lived a soldier in the world
beautiful and brave,
but he was a child's toy:
he was, you see, a paper soldier.

He wanted to remake the world,
so that everyone would be happy,
but himself was hanging by a thread:
he was, you see, a paper soldier.

He would gladly go—into fire and smoke,
to perish for you two times over,
but all you did was laugh at him:
he was, you see, a paper soldier.

You didn't put in trust to him
your important secrets,
and why was that?
Just because
he was a paper soldier.

Into fire? Well then, go! Will you go?
And one day he took the step,
and there burned up for nothing:
12   he was, you see, a paper soldier.

WARS

Carl Sandburg

First World War

In the old wars drum of hoofs and the beat of shod feet.
In the new wars hum of motors and the tread of rubber tires.
In the wars to come silent wheels and whirr of rods not yet
dreamed out in the heads of men.

In the old wars clutches of short swords and jabs into faces
with spears.
In the new wars long range guns and smashed walls, guns
running a spit of metal and men falling in tens and
twenties.
In the wars to come new silent deaths, new silent hurlers not
yet dreamed out in the heads of men.

In the old wars kings quarreling and thousands of men
following.
In the new wars kings quarreling and millions of men
following.
In the wars to come kings kicked under the dust and millions
of men following great causes not yet dreamed out in the
heads of men.

13

WAR SONGS

Traditional, Ojibwa

Nineteenth Century

TRANSLATED FROM THE OJIBWA BY HENRY ROWE SCHOOLCRAFT

I

Hear my voice, Birds of War!
I prepare a feast for you to feed on;
I see you cross the enemy's lines;
Like you I shall go.
I wish the swiftness of your wings:
I wish the vengeance of your claws:
I muster my friends:
I follow your flight.
Ho, you young men warriors,
Bear your angers in the place of fighting!

II

From the south they came, Birds of War—
Hark! to their passing scream.
I wish the body of the fiercest,
As swift, as cruel, as strong.
I cast my body to the chance of fighting.
Happy I shall be to lie in that place,
In that place where the fight was,
Beyond the enemy's line.

III

Here on my breast have I bled!
See—see! My battle scars!
Ye mountains, tremble at my yell!
    I strike for life.

DO NOT WEEP

Stephen Crane

1899

Do not weep, maiden, for war is kind.
Because your lover threw wild hands towards the sky
And the affrighted steed ran on alone,
Do not weep.
War is kind.

    Hoarse, booming drums of the regiment,
    Little souls who thirst for fight,
    These men were born to drill and die,
    The unexplained glory flies above them,
    Great is the battle-god, great, and his kingdom—
    A field where a thousand corpses lie.

Do not weep, babe, for war is kind.
Because your father tumbled in the yellow trenches,
Raged at his breast, gulped and died,
Do not weep.
War is kind.

    Swift blazing flag of the regiment,
    Eagle with crest of red and gold,
    These men were born to drill and die.
    Point for them the virtue of slaughter,
    Make plain to them the excellence of killing
    And a field where a thousand corpses lie.

Mother whose heart hung humble as a button
On the bright splendid shroud of your son,
Do not weep,
War is kind.

THE RAMBLING SOLDIER

Traditional, English

Nineteenth Century

I am a soldier, blythe and gay,
That's rambled for promotion.
I've laid the French and Spaniards low;
Some miles I've crossed the ocean.
I've travelled England and Ireland, too,
I've travelled bonny Scotland through,
I have caused some pretty girls to rue,
I'm a roving, rambling soldier.

When I was young and in my prime
Twelve years I was recruiting
Through England, Ireland, and Scotland, too,
Wherever it was suiting.
I led a gay and splendid life,
In every town a different wife;
And seldom was there any strife
With the roving, rambling soldier.

In Woolwich town I courted Jane,
Her sister and her mother;
I mean to say, when I was there,
They were jealous of each other.
Our orders came, I had to start,
I left poor Jane with a broken heart,
Then straight to Colchester did depart,
The roving, rambling soldier.

The king permission granted me
To range the country over,
From Colchester to Liverpool,
From Plymouth down to Dover;
And in whatever town I went,
To court all damsels I was bent,
And marry none was my intent,
But live a rambling soldier.

With the blooming lasses in each town
No man was ever bolder;
I thought that I was doing right,
As the king did want young soldiers.
I told them tales of fond delight,
I kept recruiting day and night,
And when I had made all things right,
Off went the rambling soldier.

And now the wars are at an end
I am not ashamed to mention
The king has given me my discharge
And granted me a pension.
No doubt some lasses will me blame,
But never once they can me shame,
And if you want to know my name,
It's Bill, the rambling soldier.

"PICK A FERN, PICK A FERN"

Bunno

Eleventh Century B.C.

TRANSLATED FROM THE CHINESE BY EZRA POUND

Pick a fern, pick a fern, ferns are high,
"Home," I'll say: home, the year's gone by,
no house, no roof, these huns on the hoof.
Work, work, work, that's how it runs,
We are here because of these huns.

Pick a fern, pick a fern, soft as they come,
I'll say "Home."
Hungry all of us, thirsty here,
no home news for nearly a year.

Pick a fern, pick a fern, if they scratch,
I'll say "Home," what's the catch?
I'll say "Go home," now October's come.
King wants us to give it all,
no rest, spring, summer, winter, fall,
Sorrow to us, sorrow to you.
We won't get out of here till we're through.

When it's cherry-time with you,
we'll see the captain's car go thru,
four big horses to pull that load.
That's what comes along our road,
What do you call three fights a month,
and won 'em all?

18

Four car-horses strong and tall
and the boss who can drive 'em all
as we slog along beside his car,
ivory bow-tips and shagreen case
to say nothing of what we face
sloggin' along in the Hien-yün war.

Willows were green when we set out,
it's blowin' an' snowin' as we go
down this road, muddy and slow,
hungry and thirsty and blue as doubt
(no one feels half of what we know).

FROM A GERMAN WAR PRIMER

Bertolt Brecht

Second World War

TRANSLATED FROM THE GERMAN BY H. R. HAYS

When the leaders speak of peace
The common folk know
That war is coming.

When the leaders curse war
The mobilisation order is already written out.

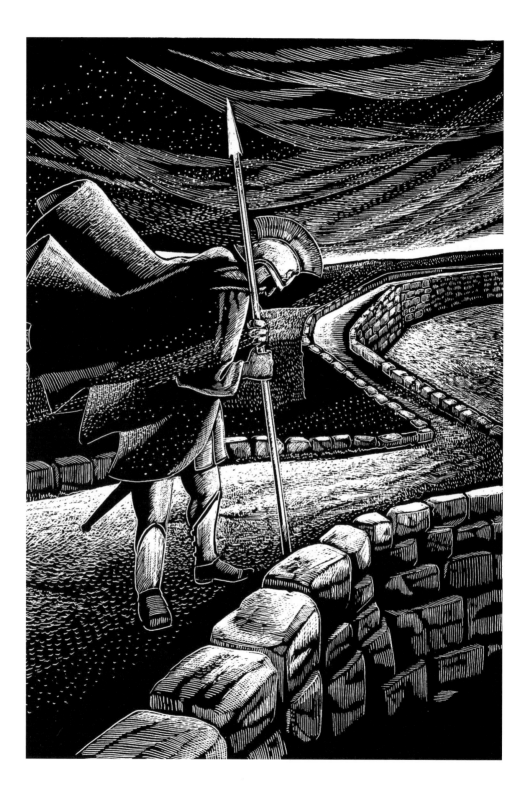

ROMAN WALL BLUES

W. H. Auden

1937, referring to the Roman occupation of Britain. Hadrian's Wall between England and Scotland was built 120–123 A.D.

Over the heather the wet wind blows,
I've lice in my tunic and a cold in my nose.

The rain comes pattering out of the sky,
I'm a Wall soldier, I don't know why.

The mist creeps over the hard grey stone,
My girl's in Tungria; I sleep alone.

Aulus goes hanging around her place,
I don't like his manners, I don't like his face.

Piso's a Christian, he worships a fish;
There'd be no kissing if he had his wish.

She gave me a ring but I diced it away;
I want my girl and I want my pay.

When I'm a veteran with only one eye
I shall do nothing but look at the sky.

THE FEMALE DRUMMER

Traditional, English

Napoleonic Wars

A maiden I was at the age of fifteen;
From my friends ran away and a soldier I became.
I 'listed in a regiment, a drummer I became,
And I learnt for to beat upon a drum-a-dum-dum-dum.

It's many a prank I've seen in the field,
And many a Frenchman I have forced for to yield;
Many's the slaughter I have seen of the French,
And so boldly I fought when I was but a wench.

A fighting top gallant in my time I have been
With the noble Duke of York at the siege of Valenciennes;
Favoured by my officers, for fear I should be slain,
They sent me to old England recruiting back again.

My hat and my feather if you had but seen
You'd thought and have sworn that a man I had been;
The drummers they enjoyed me with my fingers long and
  small,
And I played upon the row-de-dow the best of them all.

And every night to my quarters when I came,
I was no ways ashamed to lie with a man;
In pulling off my breeches to myself I often smiled,
To think I lie with a man and a maiden all the while.

They sent me to London to keep guard at the Tower,
Where I might have been a maid unto this very hour.
A young girl fell in love with me, I told her I was a maid,
And she to my officers the secret conveyed.

The officer he sent for me to know if it was true,
"For such a thing can scarcely be believed of you."
When I told him of it he smiled to me and said,
" 'Tis a pity we should lose such a drummer as you made.

"And for your noble courage at the siege of Valenciennes
A bounty shall be allowed you, my girl, from the queen."
Now I've got a husband and a drummer he became;
I have learnt him to beat upon the drum-a-dum-dum-dum.

Here's a health to the duke and a health to you,
A health to every boy that sticks to his colours true;
And if the duke is short of men before the French are slain,
So boldly I will march to fight for him again.

THE CORSICAN MONSTER

Anon., English

Napoleonic Wars

Good people all I pray give ear to what I have to tell
It is of as great a monster, as ever sprung out of hell
Perhaps you would wish to know what monster it is I mean,
He's of the breed of Corsica, and in France is to be seen,
Bonaparte is his name, and he's rightly named indeed
For the hardest bone that ever was can't his hard heart
    exceed,
Most of the nations round they do him dread we know
But at last he will be found to be only a bug-a-bow.
Many are the countries, cities, and fine towns
To his disgrace he's laid waste for his cruelty has no bounds,
The widows and the fatherless and the aged parents
He's left them all in great distress that savage Bug-a-bow,
For now with all his mighty host he means to invade our
    land,
But before he reaches to our coast we'll put him to a stand;
But if he should be so mad as to land upon our coast
We'll make him wish he never had, with all his hellish host.
For then our bull we will let loose and in his mad career,
He will run at all without excuse that dare him to come near
Over hedge and ditch he'll jump and skip so furiously he'll go
He'll not return till with his horn he's gored the Bug-a-bow
But when he'll come no one can tell it may be in the night,
Appearing like a Bug-a-bow, to put you in a fright
But if the case it should be such as perhaps it may be so
They will find our bull an over match for their barking
    Bug-a-bow.

bug-a-bow: *bogeyman*
our bull: *Englishmen were known as "John Bull"*

NAPOLEON

Walter de la Mare

1906

"What is the world, O soldiers?
    It is I:
I, this incessant snow,
  This northern sky;
Soldiers, this solitude
  Through which we go
      Is I."

BONEY

Traditional, English

Napoleonic Wars

Oh Boney was a warrior
oh weigh heigh ya
a warrior and a terrior
John Browns war

Boney went acruising
oh weigh heigh ya
in the channel of old England
John Browns war

Nelson went also acruising
oh weigh heigh ya
he fought with noble Boney
John Browns war

He got sent to Saint Helena
oh weigh heigh ya
there he died a prisoner
John Browns war

John Browns war: *a corruption of*
John François—"Johnny Frenchman"

THE CHARGE OF THE LIGHT BRIGADE

Alfred, Lord Tennyson

Crimean War

I
Half a league, half a league,
  Half a league onward,
All in the valley of Death
  Rode the six hundred.
"Forward, the Light Brigade!
Charge for the guns!" he said:
Into the valley of Death
  Rode the six hundred.

II
"Forward, the Light Brigade!"
Was there a man dismay'd?
Not tho' the soldier knew
  Some one had blunder'd:
Their's not to make reply,
Their's not to reason why,
Their's but to do and die:
Into the valley of Death
  Rode the six hundred.

III
Cannon to right of them,
Cannon to left of them,
Cannon in front of them
  Volley'd and thunder'd;
Storm'd at with shot and shell,
Boldly they rode and well,
Into the jaws of Death,
Into the mouth of Hell
  Rode the six hundred.

IV
Flash'd all their sabres bare,
Flash'd as they turn'd in air
Sabring the gunners there,
Charging an army, while
    All the world wonder'd:
Plunged in the battery-smoke
Right thro' the line they broke;
Cossack and Russian
Reel'd from the sabre-stroke
    Shatter'd and sunder'd.
Then they rode back, but not,
    Not the six hundred.

V
Cannon to right of them,
Cannon to left of them,
Cannon behind them
    Volley'd and thunder'd;
Storm'd at with shot and shell,
While horse and hero fell,
They that had fought so well
Came thro' the jaws of Death,
Back from the mouth of Hell,
All that was left of them,
    Left of six hundred.

VI
When can their glory fade?
O the wild charge they made!
    All the world wonder'd.
Honour the charge they made!
Honour the Light Brigade,
    Noble six hundred!

JOHN BROWN'S BODY

Anon., American

American Civil War

ATTRIBUTED TO CHARLES SPRAGUE HALL AND TO THOMAS BRIGHAM BISHOP

John Brown's body lies a-mould'ring in the grave,
John Brown's body lies a-mould'ring in the grave,
John Brown's body lies a-mould'ring in the grave,
   His soul goes marching on!

Chorus:
   Glory, glory! Hallelujah!
   Glory, glory! Hallelujah!
   Glory, glory! Hallelujah!
   His soul is marching on!

He captured Harper's Ferry with his nineteen men so true,
And he frightened old Virginia till she trembled through and
   through.
They hung him for a traitor, themselves the traitor crew,
   But his soul is marching on!

John Brown died that the slave might be free,
John Brown died that the slave might be free,
John Brown died that the slave might be free,
   And his soul is marching on!

The stars of Heaven are looking kindly down,
The stars of Heaven are looking kindly down,
The stars of Heaven are looking kindly down,
   On the grave of old John Brown.

Now has come the glorious jubilee,
Now has come the glorious jubilee,
Now has come the glorious jubilee,
   When all mankind are free.

CAVALRY CROSSING A FORD

Walt Whitman

American Civil War

A line in long array where they wind betwixt green islands,
They take a serpentine course, their arms flash in the sun—
    hark to the musical clank,
Behold the silvery river, in it the splashing horses loitering
    stop to drink,
Behold the brown-faced men, each group, each person a
    picture, the negligent rest on the saddles,
Some emerge on the opposite bank, others are just entering
    the ford—while,
Scarlet and blue and snowy white,
The guidon flags flutter gayly in the wind.

THE COLLEGE COLONEL

Herman Melville

American Civil War

He rides at their head;
   A crutch by his saddle just slants in view,
One slung arm is in splints, you see,
   Yet he guides his strong steed—how coldly too.

He brings his regiment home—
   Not as they filed two years before,
But a remnant half-tattered, and battered, and worn,

Like castaway sailors, who—stunned
    By the surf's loud roar,
   Their mates dragged back and seen no more—
Again and again breast the surge,
   And at last crawl, spent, to shore.

A still rigidity and pale—
   An Indian aloofness lones his brow;
He has lived a thousand years
Compressed in battle's pains and prayers,
   Marches and watches slow.

There are welcoming shouts, and flags;
   Old men off hat to the Boy,
Wreaths from gay balconies fall at his feet,
   But to *him*—there comes alloy.

It is not that a leg is lost,
   It is not that an arm is maimed,
It is not that the fever has racked—
   Self he has long disclaimed.

But all through the Seven Days' Fight,
   And deep in the Wilderness grim,
And in the field-hospital tent,
   And Petersburg crater, and dim
Lean brooding in Libby, there came—
   Ah heaven!—what *truth* to him.

LEAVING FOR THE FRONT

Alfred Lichtenstein

First World War

TRANSLATED FROM THE GERMAN BY PATRICK BRIDGWATER

Before I die I must just find this rhyme.
Be quiet, my friends, and do not waste my time.

We're marching off in company with death.
I only wish my girl would hold her breath.

There's nothing wrong with me. I'm glad to leave.
Now mother's crying too. There's no reprieve.

And now look how the sun's begun to set.
A nice mass-grave is all that I shall get.

Once more the good old sunset's glowing red.
In thirteen days I'll probably be dead.

*This poem was written on 7 August 1914—seven weeks later
Lichtenstein was dead.*

"ALL THE HILLS AND VALES ALONG"

Charles Hamilton Sorley

First World War

All the hills and vales along
Earth is bursting into song,
And the singers are the chaps
Who are going to die perhaps.
  O sing, marching men,
  Till the valleys ring again.
  Give your gladness to earth's keeping,
  So be glad, when you are sleeping.

Cast away regret and rue,
Think what you are marching to.
Little live, great pass.
Jesus Christ and Barabbas
Were found the same day.
This died, that went his way.
  So sing with joyful breath.
  For why, you are going to death.
  Teeming earth will surely store
  All the gladness that you pour.

Earth that never doubts nor fears,
Earth that knows of death, not tears,
Earth that bore with joyful ease
Hemlock for Socrates,
Earth that blossomed and was glad
'Neath the cross that Christ had,
Shall rejoice and blossom too
When the bullet reaches you.
  Wherefore, men marching
  On the road to death, sing!
  Pour your gladness on earth's head,
  So be merry, so be dead.

From the hills and valleys earth
Shouts back the sound of mirth,
Tramp of feet and lilt of song
Ringing all the road along
All the music of their going,
Ringing swinging glad song-throwing,
Earth will echo still, when foot
Lies numb and voice mute.
   On marching men, on
   To the gates of death with song.
   Sow your gladness for earth's reaping,
   So you may be glad, though sleeping.
   Strew your gladness on earth's bed,
   So be merry, so be dead.

THE SEND-OFF

Wilfred Owen

First World War

Down the close, darkening lanes they sang their way
To the siding-shed,
And lined the train with faces grimly gay.

Their breasts were struck all white with wreath and spray
As men's are, dead.

Dull porters watched them, and a casual tramp
Stood staring hard,
Sorry to miss them from the upland camp.
Then, unmoved, signals nodded, and a lamp
Winked to the guard.

So secretly, like wrongs hushed-up, they went.
They were not ours:
We never heard to which front these were sent.

Nor there if they yet mock what women meant
Who gave them flowers.

Shall they return to beatings of great bells
In wild train-loads?
A few, a few, too few for drums and yells,
May creep back, silent, to still village wells
Up half-known roads.

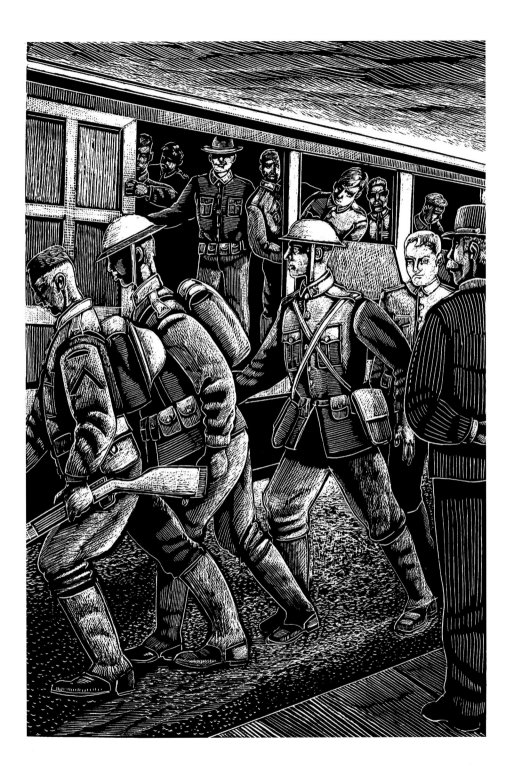

BEFORE ACTION

Leon Gellert

First World War

We always had to do our work at night.
I wondered why we had to be so sly.
I wondered why we couldn't have our fight
Under the open sky.

I wondered why I always felt so cold.
I wondered why the orders seemed so slow,
So slow to come, so whisperingly told,
So whisperingly low.

I wondered if my packing-straps were tight,
And wondered why I wondered. Sound went wild ...
An order came ... I ran into the night
Wondering why I smiled.

NO ONE CARES LESS THAN I

Edward Thomas

First World War

"No one cares less than I,
Nobody knows but God,
Whether I am destined to lie
Under a foreign clod,"
Were the words I made to the bugle call in the morning.

But laughing, storming, scorning,
Only the bugles know
What the bugles say in the morning,
And they do not care, when they blow
38 The call that I heard and made words to early this morning.

CALLIGRAM, 15 MAY 1915

Guillaume Apollinaire

First World War

TRANSLATED FROM THE FRENCH BY OLIVER BERNARD

The sky's as blue and black as ink
My eyes drown in it and sink

Darkness a shell whines over me
I write this under a willow tree

LAMENTATIONS

Siegfried Sassoon

First World War

I found him in the guard-room at the Base.
From the blind darkness I had heard his crying
And blundered in. With puzzled, patient face
A sergeant watched him; it was no good trying
To stop it; for he howled and beat his chest.
And, all because his brother had gone west,
Raved at the bleeding war; his rampant grief
Moaned, shouted, sobbed, and choked, while he was
  kneeling
Half-naked on the floor. In my belief
Such men have lost all patriotic feeling.

"HERE DEAD LIE WE BECAUSE WE DID NOT CHOOSE"

A. E. Housman

First World War

Here dead lie we because we did not choose
  To live and shame the land from which we sprung.
Life, to be sure, is nothing much to lose;
  But young men think it is, and we were young.

THE SILENT ONE

Ivor Gurney

First World War

Who died on the wires, and hung there, one of two—
Who for his hours of life had chattered through
Infinite lovely chatter of Bucks accent:
Yet faced unbroken wires; stepped over, and went
A noble fool, faithful to his stripes—and ended.
But I weak, hungry, and willing only for the chance
Of line—to fight in the line, lay down under unbroken
Wires, and saw the flashes and kept unshaken,
Till the politest voice—a finicking accent, said:
"Do you think you might crawl through there: there's a
    hole."
Darkness, shot at: I smiled, as politely replied—
"I'm afraid not, Sir." There was no hole no way to be seen
Nothing but chance of death, after tearing of clothes.
Kept flat, and watched the darkness, hearing bullets
    whizzing—
And thought of music—and swore deep heart's deep oaths
(Polite to God) and retreated and came on again,
Again retreated—and a second time faced the screen.

IN MEMORIAM (EASTER, 1915)

Edward Thomas

First World War

The flowers left thick at nightfall in the wood
This Eastertide call into mind the men,
Now far from home, who, with their sweethearts, should
Have gathered them and will do never again.

HANGING ON THE OLD BARBED WIRE

Traditional, English

First World War

If you want to find the Colonel I know where he is,
  I know where he is, I know where he is,
If you want to find the Colonel I know where he is,
  He's pinning another medal on his chest.

  chorus:
        I've seen him, I've seen him
        Pinning another medal on his chest
        I've seen him,
        Pinning another medal on his chest.

If you want to find the captain I know where he is,
  He's home again on seven days' leave.

If you want to find the quartermaster I know where he is,
  He's drinking up the company's rum.

If you want to find the sergeant I know where he is,
  He's drunk upon the dug-out floor.

If you want to find the privates I know where they are,
  I know where they are, I know where they are.
If you want to find the privates I know where they are,
  They're hanging on the old barbed wire.

  chorus:
        I've seen them, I've seen them
        Hanging on the old barbed wire
        I've seen them,
        Hanging on the old barbed wire.

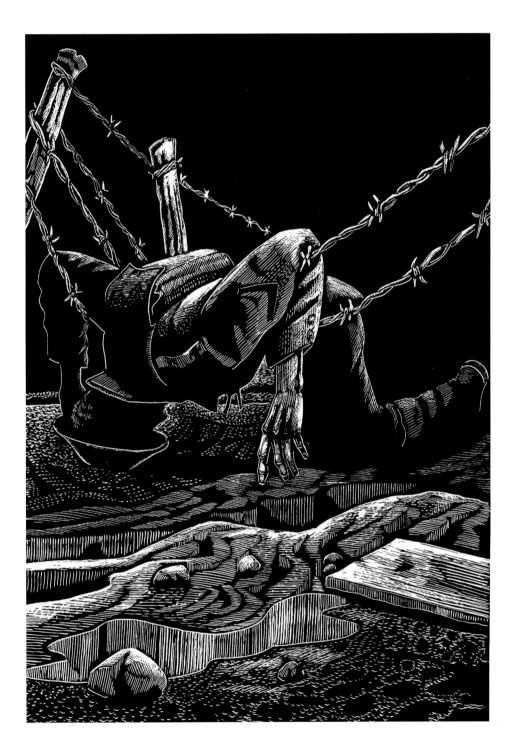

THE CHILDREN, 1914–18

Rudyard Kipling

First World War

These were our children who died for our lands: they were
  dear in our sight.
  We have only the memory left of their home-treasured
    sayings and laughter.
  The price of our loss shall be paid to our hands, not
    another's hereafter.
Neither the Alien nor Priest shall decide on it. That is our
  right.
    But who shall return us the children?

At the hour the Barbarian chose to disclose his pretences,
  And raged against Man, they engaged, on the breasts that
    they bared for us,
  The first felon-stroke of the sword he had long-time
    prepared for us—
Their bodies were all our defence while we wrought our
  defences.

They bought us anew with their blood, forbearing to blame
  us,
Those hours which we had not made good when the
  Judgment o'ercame us.
They believed us and perished for it. Our statecraft, our
  learning
Delivered them bound to the Pit and alive to the burning
Whither they mirthfully hastened as jostling for honour—
Not since her birth has our Earth seen such worth loosed
  upon her.

Nor was their agony brief, or once only imposed on them.
  The wounded, the war-spent, the sick received no
    exemption:
  Being cured they returned and endured and achieved our
    redemption,
Hopeless themselves of relief, till Death, marvelling, closed
    on them.

That flesh we had nursed from the first in all cleanness was
    given
To corruption unveiled and assailed by the malice of
    Heaven—
By the heart-shaking jests of Decay where it lolled on the
    wires—
To be blanched or gay-painted by fumes—to be cindered by
    fires—
To be senselessly tossed and retossed in stale mutilation
From crater to crater. For this we shall take expiation.
  But who shall return us our children?

"WHEN YOU SEE MILLIONS OF THE MOUTHLESS DEAD"

Charles Hamilton Sorley

First World War

When you see millions of the mouthless dead
Across your dreams in pale battalions go,
Say not soft things as other men have said,
That you'll remember. For you need not so.
Give them not praise. For, deaf, how should they know
It is not curses heaped on each gashed head?
Nor tears. Their blind eyes see not your tears flow.
Nor honour. It is easy to be dead.
Say only this, "They are dead." Then add thereto,
"Yet many a better one has died before."
Then, scanning all the o'ercrowded mass, should you
Perceive one face that you loved heretofore,
It is a spook. None wears the face you knew.
Great death has made all his for evermore.

TO HIS LOVE

Ivor Gurney

First World War

He's gone, and all our plans
   Are useless indeed.
We'll walk no more on Cotswold
   Where the sheep feed
   Quietly and take no heed.

His body that was so quick
   Is not as you
Knew it, on Severn river
   Under the blue
   Driving our small boat through.

You would not know him now . . .
   But still he died
Nobly, so cover him over
   With violets of pride
   Purple from Severn side.

Cover him, cover him soon!
   And with thick-set
Masses of memoried flowers—
   Hide that red wet
   Thing I must somehow forget.

EPITAPHS OF THE WAR, 1914–18

Rudyard Kipling

First World War

"EQUALITY OF SACRIFICE"

A. "I was a Have." B. "I was a 'have-not.'"
     (*Together.*) "What hast thou given which I gave not?"

A SON

My son was killed while laughing at some jest. I would I
    knew
What it was, and it might serve me in a time when jests are
    few.

THE COWARD

I could not look on Death, which being known,
Men led me to him, blindfold and alone.

THE BEGINNER

On the first hour of my first day
   In the front trench I fell.
(Children in boxes at a play
   Stand up to watch it well.)

THE REFINED MAN

I was of delicate mind. I stepped aside for my needs,
   Disdaining the common office. I was seen from afar and
      killed . . .
How is this matter for mirth? Let each man be judged by his
    deeds.
   I have paid my price to live with myself on the terms that I
   willed.

COMMON FORM

If any question why we died,
Tell them, because our fathers lied.

A DEAD STATESMAN

I could not dig: I dared not rob:
Therefore I lied to please the mob.
Now all my lies are proved untrue
And I must face the men I slew.
What tale shall serve me here among
Mine angry and defrauded young?

EPITAPH

Anakreon

Sixth Century B.C.

TRANSLATED FROM THE GREEK BY PETER JAY

Timokritos was bold in war. This is his grave.
Arês the war-god spares the coward, not the brave.

CENOTAPH AT THE ISTHMOS

Simonides

Fifth Century B.C.

TRANSLATED FROM THE GREEK BY PETER JAY

We did not flinch but gave our lives to save
Greece when her fate hung on a razor's edge.

THERMOPYLAE

Simonides

480 B.C.

TRANSLATED FROM THE GREEK BY WILLIAM LISLE BOWLES

Go tell the Spartans, thou that passest by,
That here, obedient to their laws, we lie.

"HOW FEW OF US ARE LEFT, HOW FEW!"

Anon., Chinese

c. 800–600 B.C.

TRANSLATED FROM THE CHINESE BY ARTHUR WALEY

How few of us are left, how few!
Why do we not go back?
Were it not for our prince and his concerns,
What should we be doing here in the dew?

How few of us are left, how few!
Why do we not go back?
Were it not for our prince's own concerns,
What should we be doing here in the mud?

THE TIMES

Charles Madge

Second World War

Time wasted and time spent
Daytime with used up wit
Time to stand, time to sit
Or wait and see if it
Happens, happy event.

For war is eating now.

Waking, shaking of death
Leaving the white sheets
And dull head who repeats
The dream of his defeats
And drawing colder breath

For war is eating now.

Growing older, going
Where the water runs
Black as death, and guns
Explode the singing suns
Blowing like hell, snowing

For war is eating now.

AN IRISH AIRMAN FORESEES HIS DEATH

W. B. Yeats

First World War

I know that I shall meet my fate
Somewhere among the clouds above;
Those that I fight I do not hate,
Those that I guard I do not love;
My country is Kiltartan Cross,
My countrymen Kiltartan's poor,
No likely end could bring them loss
Or leave them happier than before.
Nor law, nor duty bade me fight,
Nor public men, nor cheering crowds,

A lonely impulse of delight
Drove to this tumult in the clouds;
I balanced all, brought all to mind,
The years to come seemed waste of breath,
A waste of breath the years behind
In balance with this life, this death.

SO MANY TIMES I'VE SEEN . . .

Yuliya Drunina

Second World War

TRANSLATED FROM THE RUSSIAN BY ALBERT C. TODD

So many times I've seen hand-to-hand combat.
Once for real, and a thousand times in dreams.
Whoever says that war is not horrible,
Knows nothing about war.

A BURNT SHIP

John Donne

1590s

Out of a fired ship, which, by no way
But drowning, could be rescued from the flame,
Some men leaped forth, and ever as they came
Near the foe's ships, did by their shot decay;
So all were lost, which in the ship were found,
   They in the sea being burnt, they in the burnt ship drowned.

CONVOY

Charles Causley

Second World War

Draw the blanket of ocean
Over the frozen face.
He lies, his eyes quarried by glittering fish,
Staring through the green freezing sea-glass
At the Northern Lights.

He is now a child in the land of Christmas:
Watching, amazed, the white tumbling bears
And the diving seal.
The iron wind clangs round the ice-caps,
The five-pointed Dog-star
Burns over the silent sea,

And the three ships
Come sailing in.

WHEN A BEAU GOES IN

Gavin Ewart

Second World War

When a Beau goes in,
Into the drink,
It makes you think,
Because, you see, they always sink
But nobody says "Poor lad"
Or goes about looking sad
Because, you see, it's war,
It's the unalterable law.

Although it's perfectly certain
The pilot's gone for a Burton
And the observer too
It's nothing to do with you
And if they both should go
To a land where falls no rain nor hail nor driven snow—
Here, there or anywhere,
Do you suppose *they* care?

You shouldn't cry
Or say a prayer or sigh.
In the cold sea, in the dark,
It isn't a lark
But it isn't Original Sin—
It's just a Beau going in.

SONG OF THE DYING GUNNER AA1

Charles Causley

Second World War

[HMS Glory]

Oh mother my mouth is full of stars
As cartridges in the tray
My blood is a twin-branched scarlet tree
And it runs all runs away.

Oh "Cooks to the galley" is sounded off
And the lads are down in the mess
But I lie done by the forrard gun
With a bullet in my breast.

Don't send me a parcel at Christmas time
Of socks and nutty and wine
And don't depend on a long weekend
By the Great Western Railway line.

Farewell, Aggie Weston, the Barracks at Guz,
Hang my tiddley suit on the door
I'm sewn up neat in a canvas sheet
And I shan't be home no more.

AA1: *Anti-Aircraft Gunner, 1st Class*
Aggie Weston: *the familiar term used by sailors to describe the hostels
    founded in many seaports by Dame Agnes Weston*
Guz: *naval slang for Devonport*
tiddley suit: *sailor's best shore-going uniform with gold badges*

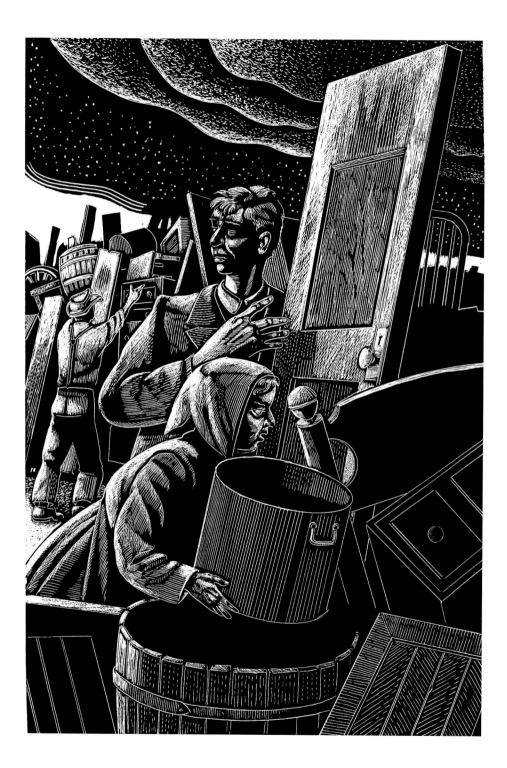

BUILDING THE BARRICADE

Anna Świrszczyńska

Second World War

TRANSLATED FROM THE POLISH BY MAGNUS JAN KRYNSKI AND ROBERT MAGUIRE

We were afraid as we built the barricade
under fire.

The tavern-keeper, the jeweller's mistress, the barber,
all of us cowards.

The servant-girl fell to the ground
as she lugged a paving stone, we were terribly afraid
all of us cowards—
the janitor, the market-woman, the pensioner.

The pharmacist fell to the ground
as he dragged the door of a toilet,
we were even more afraid, the smuggler-woman,
the dressmaker, the streetcar driver,
all of us cowards.

A kid from reform school fell
as he dragged a sandbag,
you see we were really
afraid.

Though no one forced us,
we did build the barricade
under fire.

THE HOUSE THAT FEAR BUILT: WARSAW, 1943

Jane Flanders

Second World War

THE PURPOSE OF POETRY IS TO REMIND US
HOW DIFFICULT IT IS TO REMAIN JUST ONE PERSON,
FOR OUR HOUSE IS OPEN, THERE ARE NO KEYS IN THE DOORS.—CZESLAW MILOSZ

I am the boy with his hands raised over his head
in Warsaw.

I am the soldier whose rifle is trained
on the boy with his hands raised over his head
in Warsaw.

I am the woman with lowered gaze
who fears the soldier whose rifle is trained
on the boy with his hands raised over his head
in Warsaw.

I am the man in the overcoat
who loves the woman with lowered gaze
who fears the soldier whose rifle is trained
on the boy with his hands raised over his head
in Warsaw.

I am the stranger who photographs
the man in the overcoat
who loves the woman with lowered gaze
who fears the soldier whose rifle is trained
on the boy with his hands raised over his head
in Warsaw.

The crowd, of which I am each part, moves on
beneath my window, for I am the crone too
who shakes her sheets
over every street in the world
muttering
What's this? What's this?

WRITTEN IN PENCIL IN THE SEALED RAILWAY-CAR

Dan Pagis

Second World War

TRANSLATED FROM THE HEBREW BY STEPHEN MITCHELL

here in this carload
i am eve
with abel my son
if you see my other son
cain son of man
tell him i

"DON'T BE AFRAID"

David Vogel

Second World War

TRANSLATED FROM THE HEBREW BY T. CARMI

Don't be afraid, my child, those are
only two mice, jumping down from the
table to the chair. They are smaller
than you and couldn't gobble you up.

Don't be afraid, my child, that's only
the rain's finger tapping wetly on the
window. We won't let it in.

Hide deep inside me, I am your mother.
We'll pull the dark night over our
heads and no one will find us.

61

THE CHILDREN'S EXODUS

Karen Gershon

1966, remembering 1938

I
It was an ordinary train
travelling across Germany
which gathered and took us away
those who saw us may have thought
that it was for a holiday
not being exiled being taught
to hate what we had loved in vain
brought us lasting injury

II
Our parents let us go
knowing that who stayed must die
but kept the truth from us although
they gave us to reality
did they consider what it meant
to become orphaned and not know
to be emotionally freed
when our childhood seeds were spent

III
When we went out of Germany
carrying six million lives
that was Jewish history
but each child was one refugee
we unlike the Egyptian slaves
were exiled individually
and each in desolation has
created his own wilderness

62

This race-hatred was personal
IV we were condemned for what we were
no one escaped the ritual
from which we rose inferior
the blood-guilt entered every home
till daily life was a pogrom
we who were there are not the same
as those who have no wreck to share

Home is where some know who you are
V the rescue was impersonal
it was no one's concern what use
we made of the years given us
one should not ask of children who
find their survival natural
gratitude for being where
ten thousand others have come too

At Dovercourt the winter sea
VI was like God's mercy vast and wild
a fever to a land-locked child
it seemed fire and cloud to me
the world's blood and my blood were cold
the exiled Jew in me was old
and thoughts of death appalled me less
than knowledge of my loneliness

My mother sold my bed and chair
VII while I expected to return
yet she had kept me close to her
till I saw our temple burn
it was not for her sake but mine
she knew that I was unripe fruit
and that exile was a blight
against which one prepared in vain

VIII   People at Dovercourt were gay
as if they thought we could forget
our homes in alien play
as if we were not German Jews
but mealtimes were a market place
when sudden visitors could choose
although we were not orphaned yet
a son or daughter by their face

IX   My childhood smoulders in the name
of the town which was my home
all we were became no more
than answers on a questionnaire
at Dovercourt we were taught that
our share of the Jewish fate
had not been left behind but was
the refugee life facing us

WAR HAS BEEN GIVEN A BAD NAME

Bertolt Brecht

Second World War

TRANSLATED FROM THE GERMAN BY JOHN WILLETT

I am told that the best people have begun saying
How, from a moral point of view, the Second World War
Fell below the standard of the First. The Wehrmacht
Allegedly deplores the methods by which the SS effected
The extermination of certain peoples. The Ruhr industrialists
Are said to regret the bloody manhunts
Which filled their mines and factories with slave workers. The
   intellectuals
So I heard, condemn industry's demand for slave workers
Likewise their unfair treatment. Even the bishops
Dissociate themselves from this way of waging war; in short
   the feeling
Prevails in every quarter that the Nazis did the Fatherland
A lamentably bad turn, and that war
While in itself natural and necessary, has, thanks to the
Unduly uninhibited and positively inhuman
Way in which it was conducted on this occasion, been
Discredited for some time to come.

WHAT WAS LOST

W. B. Yeats

1930s

I sing what was lost and dread what was won,
I walk in a battle fought over again,
My king a lost king, and lost soldiers my men;
Feet to the Rising and Setting may run,
They always beat on the same small stone.

JUNGLE NIGHT

"K"

Second World War, Burma

The man with the green cigarette strolls down the path
Waving it in the air in conversation.
The man with the tiny anvil strikes it softly like a bell—
Tink-tink; tink-tink.
The man with the dark blue cloak goes quietly by.
There goes the man with the green cigarette again.

They are not really there. You know quite well
They are not there.
Then one of them whistles softly
You finger the trigger of your Bren.

Half-fearing, half-desiring the sudden hell
Pressure will loose.
You listen—
Nothing—
Then

The man with the green cigarette strolls by again
Waving it in the air.
Down comes the dew,
Drip-drip; drip-drip.
The man with the tiny silver anvil
Strikes twice; strikes twice
Softly passes the man with the cloak of blue.

Fireflies.
Bell birds
Shadows
Japanese.

THE MYTH OF HIROSHIMA

Saga Nobuyuki

Second World War

TRANSLATED FROM THE JAPANESE BY KIJIMA HAJIME

What are they looking for,
running to the summit of lost time?
Hundreds of people vaporized instantly
are walking in mid-air.

> "We didn't die."
> "We skipped over death in a flash and became spirits."
> "Give us a real, human death."

One man's shadow among hundreds is branded on stone
    steps.

> "Why am I imprisoned in stone?"
> "Where did my flesh go, separated from its shadow?"
> "What must I wait for?"

The twentieth-century myth is stamped with fire.
Who will free this shadow from the stone?

68   *The first atomic bomb was dropped on Hiroshima on 6 August 1945.*

"IN THE FIRE, A TELEGRAPH POLE"

Hara Tamiki

Second World War

TRANSLATED FROM THE JAPANESE BY GEOFFREY BOWNAS AND ANTHONY THWAITE

In the fire, a telegraph pole
At the heart of the fire.
A telegraph pole like a stamen,
Like a candle,
Blazing up, like a molten
Red stamen.
In the heart of the fire on the other bank
From this morning, one by one,
Fear has screamed
Through men's eyes. At the heart of the fire
A telegraph pole, like a stamen.

The poet committed suicide in 1951 after confirmation of the symptoms of "atom disease."

TO MY COUNTRYMEN

Bertolt Brecht

After the Second World War

TRANSLATED FROM THE GERMAN BY H. ARTHUR KLEIN

You who survive in cities that have died
Now show some mercy to yourselves at last.
Don't march, poor things, to war as in the past
As if past wars left you unsatisfied.
I beg you—mercy for yourselves at last.

You men, reach for the spade and not the knife.
You'd sit in safety under roofs today
Had you not used the knife to make your way
And under roofs one leads a better life.
I beg you, take the spade and not the knife.

You children, to be spared another war
You must speak out and tell your parents plain.
You will not live in ruins once again
Nor undergo what they've had to endure.
You children, to be spared another war.

You mothers, since the word is yours to give
To stand for war or not to stand for war
I beg you, choose to let your children live.
Let birth, not death, be what they thank you for.
You mothers, choose to let your children live.

VIETNAM

Clarence Major

Vietnam War

he was just back
from the war

said man they got
whites

over there now
fighting
us

and blacks over there
too

fighting us

and we can't tell
our whites
from the others

nor our blacks
from the others

& everybody
is just killing

& killing
like crazy

HELL NO! I AIN'T GONNA GO!

Matthew Jones & Elaine Lavon

Vietnam War

Up tight! That's right!
I ain't gonna go! Hell no!
    I ain't goin' to Vietnam,
    I ain't dyin' for Uncle Sam.
Up tight! That's right!
I ain't gonna go! Hell no!
    I ain't going to Vietnam,
    I ain't burnin' my brothers to serve The Man.
Up tight! That's right!
I ain't gonna go! Hell no!
    I ain't goin' to Vietnam,
    The Viet-cong's just like I am.
Up tight! Up tight! Up tight!
    Let's run it down, brother Brown,
    Tell every cat just where it's at,
    I've had enough of Charlie's stuff,
    If he messes with me I'm gonna get rough.
Up tight! That's right!
I ain't gonna go! Hell no!

CENTRAL HIGHLANDS, VIET NAM, 1968

Geary Hobson

Vietnam War

I
An eagle glides above the plain
where mice scurry in a vortex
of smoke and blood.
Wings dip, soar downward
in a clash
of fire
and upheaval
of earth and bone.

II
You will die, Dull Knife,
and your people,
and your vanquisher's descendants
will weep over their father's deeds.

III
In the mountains of Viet Nam
the Meo people, too,
will pass
from this world in napalm flashes
and burnt-out hillsides
and all that will be left
to give
will be
the helpless tears
of history future.

IV
The eagle flies blindly
into the smoke of his past.

MANUEL IS QUIET SOMETIMES

Martín Espada

Vietnam War

He was quiet again,
driving east on 113,
near the slaughterhouse
on the day after Christmas,
not mourning,
but almost bowed,
like it is after the funeral
of a distant relative,
thoughtful,
sorrow on the border at dusk.

Vietnam was a secret.
Some men there collected cars,
some gold teeth.
Manuel collected the moist silences
between bursts of mortar.
He would not tell
what creatures laughed in his sleep,
or what blood was still drying
from bright to dark
in moments of boredom
and waiting.
A few people knew
about the wound,
a jabbing in his leg
(though he refused
to limp);
I knew about the time
he went AWOL.

Driving east on 113,
he talked
about how he keeps
the car running
in winter. It's

a good car,
he said.
There was the brief illumination
of passing headlights,
and slaughterhouse smoke
halted in the sky.

Another night,
the night of the Chicano dance,
Manuel's head swung slow and lazy
with drinking.
He smiled repeatedly,
a polite amnesiac,
and drank other people's beer,
waiting for the dancers
to leave their tables
so he could steal the residue
in plastic cups.

It was almost 2 AM
when he toppled,
aimless as something beheaded,
collapsing so he huddled
a prisoner on the floor.

The shell of his body
swung elbows
when we pulled him up.
He saw me first,
seeing a stranger.
His eyes were the color
of etherized dreams,
eyes that could
castrate the enemy,
easy murder watching me
with no reflection.

This is what he said:
"I never lied
to you, man."

VAPOR TRAIL
REFLECTED IN THE FROG POND

Galway Kinnell

Vietnam War

I
The old watch: their
thick eyes
puff and foreclose by the moon. The young, heads
trailed by the beginnings of necks,
shiver,
in the guarantee they shall be bodies.

In the frog pond
the vapor trail of a SAC bomber creeps,

I hear its drone, drifting, high up
in immaculate ozone.

II
And I hear,
coming over the hills, America singing,
her varied carols I hear:
crack of deputies' rifles practicing their aim on stray dogs at
    night,
sput of cattleprod,
TV groaning at the smells of the human body,
curses of the soldier as he poisons, burns, grinds, and stabs
the rice of the world,
with open mouth, crying strong, hysterical curses.

And by rice paddies in Asia

III bones
wearing a few shadows
walk down a dirt road, smashed
bloodsuckers on their heel, knowing
the flesh a man throws down in the sunshine
dogs shall eat
and the flesh that is upthrown in the air
shall be seized by birds,
shoulder blades smooth, unmarked by old feather-holes,
hands rivered
by blue, erratic wanderings of the blood,
eyes crinkled up
as they gaze up at the drifting sun that gives us our lives,
seed dazzled over the footbattered blaze of the earth.

CAMBODIA

James Fenton

Cambodian War

One man shall smile one day and say goodbye.
Two shall be left, two shall be left to die.

One man shall give his best advice.
Three men shall pay the price.

One man shall live, live to regret.
Four men shall meet the debt.

One man shall wake from terror to his bed.
Five men shall be dead.

One man to five. A million men to one.
And still they die. And still the war goes on.

FOR A FRIEND WHO WAS KILLED IN THE WAR

Mazisi Kunene

1970

Single Voice:	In the sun-drenched cliffs of the evening
	Where I bade my brother farewell.
Group:	Birds beat their wings and turn away.
Single Voice:	I should not have returned alive
Group:	The heart weeps endlessly.
Single Voice:	It would have been you facing this fatal grief.
All:	The worlds have scars, the worlds weep.
Single Voice:	Even the dreams that I dream fill me with fear.
All:	The leopard devours whom it chooses,
	It is now I experience the grief of widows.
Single Voice:	How shall I report at the house of Somhlalela?
	How shall I?

GUNS

Sa'di Yusuf

Beirut, 1982

TRANSLATED FROM THE ARABIC BY ABDULLAH AL-UDHARI

The guns roar at dawn
And the sea enfolds the city like smoke
The guns roar at dawn
And the birds are frightened
Have the planes come?

In an empty flat
The plants are silent
The vase is shaking

ESSENTIAL SERBO-CROAT

Ken Smith

1993

Guraj	Push
Pomozi mi	Help me
Boli	It hurts
Boli me	I have a pain
Boli me ovdje	I have a pain here
Bole me grudi	I have a pain in my breast
Bole me prsa	I have a pain in my chest
Boli me oko	I have a pain in my eye
Boli me stopalo	I have a pain in my foot
Boli me glava	I have a pain in my head
Hitno je	It's urgent
Ozbiljno je	It's serious
Boli me ovdje	It hurts here
Boli puno	It hurts a lot
To je jaka bol	It's a sharp pain
To je mrtva bol	It's a dull pain
To je uporna bol	It's a nagging pain
Vecinom vremena	Most of the time
Vrti mi se u glavi	I feel dizzy
Zlo mi je	I feel sick
Slabo mi je	I feel weak
Nije dobro	It's no good
Izgubio sam sve	I have lost everything
Ne mogu vam pomoci	I can't help you

EPITAPH ON AN ARMY OF MERCENARIES

A. E. Housman

1922

These, in the day when heaven was falling,
  The hour when earth's foundations fled,
Followed their mercenary calling
  And took their wages and are dead.

Their shoulders held the sky suspended;
  They stood, and earth's foundations stay;
What God abandoned, these defended,
  And saved the sum of things for pay.

ANOTHER EPITAPH ON AN ARMY OF MERCENARIES

Hugh MacDiarmid

1935

It is a God-damned lie to say that these
Saved, or knew, anything worth any man's pride.
They were professional murderers and they took
Their blood money and impious risks and died.
In spite of all their kind some elements of worth
With difficulty persist here and there on earth.

BACK

Wilfrid Gibson

First World War

They ask me where I've been,
And what I've done and seen.
But what can I reply
Who know it wasn't I,
But some one just like me,
Who went across the sea
And with my head and hands
Killed men in foreign lands ...
Though I must bear the blame,
Because he bore my name.

BARBARA

Jacques Prévert

Second World War

TRANSLATED FROM THE FRENCH BY NEIL PHILIP

Remember Barbara
It rained down on Brest all that day
And you walked smiling
Radiant rapt streaming
In the rain
Remember Barbara
It rained down on Brest all that day
And I passed you on the rue de Siam
You smiled
And I smiled too
Remember Barbara
You whom I didn't know
You who didn't know me
Remember
Remember that day all the same
Don't forget
A man was sheltering in a doorway
And he called your name
Barbara
And you ran toward him in the rain
Streaming rapt radiant
And you threw yourself into his arms
Remember that Barbara
And don't be angry with me if I'm too familiar
I'm like that with everyone I love
Even if I've only seen them once
I'm like that with everyone in love
Even if I don't know them
Remember Barbara
Don't forget
That wise happy rain
On your happy face
On that happy town

That rain on the sea
On the arsenal
On the ferry to the isle of Ouessant
Oh Barbara
What a stupid mess war is
What's become of you now
Under this rain of iron
Of fire of steel of blood
And of the man who took you in his arms
Lovingly
Is he dead missing or even still alive
Oh Barbara
It's raining down on Brest
As it rained before
But it's not the same and everything is spoilt
It's a rain of grief terror loss
No longer a storm
Of iron of steel of blood
Just clouds
Like dead dogs
Which burst
Over the waterways of Brest
And disappear to rot
Away far away from Brest
Of which nothing remains

REPORT ON EXPERIENCE

Edmund Blunden

First World War

I have been young, and now am not too old;
And I have seen the righteous forsaken,
His health, his honour and his quality taken.
    This is not what we were formerly told.

I have seen a green country, useful to the race,
Knocked silly with guns and mines, its villages vanished,
Even the last rat and last kestrel banished—
    God bless us all, this was peculiar grace.

I knew Seraphina; Nature gave her hue,
Glance, sympathy, note, like one from Eden.
I saw her smile warp, heard her lyric deaden;
    She turned to harlotry;—this I took to be new.

Say what you will, our God sees how they run.
These disillusions are His curious proving
That He loves humanity and will go on loving;
    Over there are faith, life, virtue in the sun.

PHOOIE!

Robert Garioch

1971

With my girl,
watching an old movie,
I says,
"That's all wrong,"
I says.
"Those shells on the picture,"
I says,
"go Phooie-bang,"
I says,
"whereas, at the receiving-end,"
I says,
"they go Bang-phooie,"
I says,
"if you're still there to hear them coming,"
I says,
"after they've arrived, if you know what I mean,"
I says.

"Phooie!"
she says,
"I don't want to be told all that,
I just want to enjoy the movie,"
she says.

MRS. McGRATH

Traditional, Irish

Eighteenth/Nineteenth Century

Oh Mrs. McGrath, the Sergeant said,
Would you like to make a soldier out of your son Ted,
With a scarlet coat and a big cocked hat,
Now Mrs. McGrath wouldn't you like that?

chorus:
>With your too-ri-aa, fol-the-diddle-da,
>Too-ri- oo-ri oo-ri aa,
>With your too-ri-aa, fol-the-diddle-da,
>Too-ri oo-ri oo-ri aa.

Now Mrs. McGrath lived on the seashore
For the space of seven long years or more.
Till she saw a big ship sailing into the bay.
Here's my son Ted, wisha clear the way.

Oh Captain dear, where have you been,
Have you been sailing on the Mediterreen?
Or have you tidings of my son Ted?
Is the poor boy living or is he dead?

Then up comes Ted without any legs
And in their place he has two wooden pegs.
She kissed him a dozen times or so.
Saying surely to Jesus it can't be you?

Oh then were you drunk or were you blind
That you left your two fine legs behind?
Or was it walking upon the sea
Wore your two fine legs from the knees away?

No I wasn't drunk and I wasn't blind
But I left my two fine legs behind.
For a cannon ball on the fifth of May
Took my two fine legs from the knees away.

Oh then Teddy my boy, the widow cried,
Your two fine legs were your mammy's pride.
Them stumps of a tree wouldn't do at all.
Why didn't you run from the big cannon ball?

All foreign wars I do proclaim
Between Don John and the King of Spain,
And begob I'll make them rue the time
That they took the legs from a child of mine.

Oh then, if I had you back again,
I'd never let you go to fight the King of Spain,
For I'd rather my Ted as he used to be
Than the King of France and his whole Navee.

WAR

Ebenezer Elliott

Nineteenth Century

The victories of mind,
Are won for all mankind;
But war wastes what it wins,
Ends worse than it begins,
And is a game of woes,
Which nations always lose:
Though tyrant tyrant kill,
The slayer liveth still.

EVERYONE SANG

Siegfried Sassoon

End of the First World War

Everyone suddenly burst out singing;
And I was filled with such delight
As prisoned birds must find in freedom,
Winging wildly across the white
Orchards and dark-green fields; on—on—and out of sight.

Everyone's voice was suddenly lifted;
And beauty came like the setting sun:
My heart was shaken with tears; and horror
Drifted away . . . O, but Everyone
Was a bird; and the song was wordless; the singing will
    never be done.

INDEX OF POETS

INDEX OF TITLES AND FIRST LINES

Titles are in *italics*. Where the title and the first line are the same, the first line only is listed.

ACKNOWLEDGMENTS

We acknowledge permission to include the following copyright poems in this collection:

Anakreon: Untitled epitaph translated by Peter Jay from Peter Jay (ed.): *The Greek Anthology* (Penguin Books, 1973). Copyright © Peter Jay, 1973, by permission of Penguin Books Ltd.

W.H. Auden: "Roman Wall Blues" from *Collected Poems*, edited by Edward Mendelson. Copyright 1940 and renewed 1968 by W.H. Auden, by permission of the publishers, Random House, Inc and Faber & Faber Ltd.

Guillaume Apollinaire, translated by Oliver Bernard: "Calligram, 15 May 1915" from *Selected Poems* (Penguin Modern European Poets 1965), original `Le Ciel est d'un bleu profond' from *Poèmes à Madelaine* by Guillaume Apollinaire, © Editions Gallimard, 1952, by permission of Editions Gallimard.

Edmund Blunden: "Report on Experience" from *Poems of Many Years*, by permission of The Peters Fraser & Dunlop Group Ltd.

Bertolt Brecht: lines from "A German War Primer," translated by H.R. Hays, "War has been given a bad name," translated by John Willett, and "To My Countrymen," translated by H. Arthur Klein, from John Willett and Ralph Manheim (eds): *Brecht Poems 1913–1956* (Methuen, 1976), Copyright © 1976, 1979 by Methuen London, Ltd, by permission of Routledge, Inc, and Random House UK Ltd.

Bunno, translated by Ezra Pound: "Pick a fern, pick a fern" from *The Classic Anthology as Defined by Confucius* by Ezra Pound (Cambridge, Mass: Harvard University Press) Copyright © 1954, 1982 by the President and Fellows of Harvard College, by permission of the publishers, Harvard University Press and Faber & Faber Ltd.

Charles Causley: "Song of the Dying Gunner" and "Convoy" from *Collected Poems* (Macmillan), by permission of David Higham Associates.

Walter de la Mare: extract from "Napoleon" from *The Complete Poems of Walter de la Mare* (Faber, 1969), by permission of The Literary Trustees of Walter de la Mare and The Society of Authors as their representative.

Yuliya Drunina, translated by Albert C. Todd: "So Many Times I've Seen" from *20th Century Russian Poetry* by Yevgeny Yevtushenko, Copyright © 1993 by Doubleday, a division of Bantam Doubleday Dell Publishing Group, Inc, by permission of Doubleday, a division of Bantam Doubleday Dell Publishing Group, Inc.

Martín Espada: "Manuel is Quiet Sometimes" from *Trumpets from the Islands of their Eviction* (Bilingual Review Press, 1987), by permission of the author.

Gavin Ewart: "When a Beau Goes In" from *The Collected Ewart 1933–1980* (Hutchinson, 1980), by permission of Mrs Margo Ewart.

James Fenton: "Cambodia" from *The Memory of War and Children in Exile: Poems 1968–1983* (Penguin), by permission of The Peters Fraser & Dunlop Group Ltd.

Jane Flanders: "The House that Fear Built: Warsaw 1943" from *Timepiece* by Jane Flanders, © 1988, by permission of the publisher, The University of Pittsburgh Press.

Robert Garioch: "Phooie" from *The Complete Poetical Works of Robert Garioch* (Macdonald Publishing, Edinburgh, 1983) by permission of the Saltire Society.

Leon Gellert: "Before Action" from *Songs of a Campaign* (Angus & Robertson, 1917), by permission of HarperCollins Publishers, Australia.

Karen Gershon: "The Children's Exodus" from *Collected Poems* (Macmillan, 1990), by permission of the publishers.

Wilfrid Wilson Gibson: "Back" from *W.W. Gibson: Collected Poems 1905–25* (Macmillan), by permission of the publishers.

Ivor Gurney: "The Silent One" and "To His Love" from *Collected Poems of Ivor Gurney* edited by P.J. Kavanagh (OUP, 1982), copyright © Robin Haines, Sole Trustee of the Gurney Estate, 1982, by permission of Oxford University Press.

Hara Tamiki: Untitled poem ("In the fire, a telegraph pole") from *The Penguin Book of Japanese Verse* translated by Geoffrey Bownas and Anthony Thwaite (Penguin Books, 1964), translation Copyright © Geoffrey Bownas and Anthony Thwaite, 1964, by permission of Penguin Books Ltd.

Geary Hobson: "Central Highlands, Viet Nam, 1968" from *Deerhunting and Other Poems* (Strawberry Press, 1988), © 1988 by Geary Hobson.

A.E. Housman: "Epitaph on an Army of Mercenaries" and "Here dead lie we, because we did not choose" from *The Collected Poems of A.E. Housman*, © 1939, 1940, © 1965 by Henry Holt and Company Inc, © 1967 by Robert E. Symons, by permission of Henry Holt & Company, Inc, and The Society of Authors as the Literary representative of the Estate of A.E. Housman.

Matthew Jones & Elaine Lavon: "Hell No! I Ain't Gonna Go!" from Karl Dallas (ed): *The Cruel Wars: 100 Soldiers' Songs* (Wolfe Publishing, London, 1972).

"K": "Jungle Night" from Kenneth Baker (ed): *The Faber Book of War Poetry* (1996).

Sidney Keyes: "War Poet" from *The Collected Poems of Sidney Keyes* (Routledge, 1945) by permission of the publisher.

Galway Kinnell: "Vapor Trail Reflected in the Frog Pond" from *Body Rags* by Galway Kinnell, Copyright © 1965, 1966, 1967 by Galway Kinnell, by permission of Houghton Mifflin Company. All rights reserved.

Rudyard Kipling: "The Children" and "Epitaphs of the War" from *The Definitive Edition of Rudyard Kipling's Verse* (Hodder & Stoughton), by permission of A.P. Watt Ltd on behalf of The National Trust for Places of Historic Interest or Natural Beauty.

Mazise Kunene: "For a Friend Who Was Killed in War" from *Zulu Poems* (André Deutsch Ltd, London and Africana Publishing Company, New York, 1970), Copyright © Mazise Kunene 1970.

Alfred Liechtenstein: "Leaving for the Front", translated by Patrick Bridgewater, from Jon Silkin (ed): *The Penguin Book of First World War Poetry* (2nd ed, 1981).

Hugh MacDiarmid: "Another Epitaph on an Army of Mercenaries" from *Complete Poems* (Carcanet, 1993), by permission of Carcanet Press Ltd.

Charles Madge: "The Times" from *Love, Time and Places: Selected Poems* by Charles Madge (Anvil Press Poetry, 1994), by permission of Anvil Press Poetry.

Clarence Major: "Vietnam" from *Swallow the Lake*, (Wesleyan University Press), © 1970 by Clarence Major, by permission of the University Press of New England.

Bulat Okudzhava, translated by Albert C. Todd: "Paper Soldier" from *20th Century Russian Poetry* by Yevgeny Yevtushenko, Copyright © 1993 by Doubleday, a division of Bantam Doubleday Dell Publishing Group, Inc, by permission of Doubleday, a division of Bantam Doubleday Dell Publishing Group, Inc.

Dan Pagis: "Written in Pencil in the Sealed Railway-Car" from *T. Carmi and Dan Pagis: Selected Poems*, translated by Stephen Mitchell, by permission of the publishers, Carcanet Press Ltd.

Jacques Prévert: "Barbara" from *Paroles* by Jacques Prevert, © Editions Gallimard (1949), by permission of Editions Gallimard on behalf of the author's Estate; this English translation by Neil Philip, Copyright © Neil Philip 1998.

Saga Nobuyuki, translated by Kijima Hajime: "The Myth of Hiroshima" from Kijima Hajime (ed): *The Poetry of Post War Japan* (University of Iowa Press, 1974), translation © Kijima Hajime 1974, by permission of the translator and editor.

Carl Sandburg: "Wars" from *Chicago Poems* by Carl Sandburg, copyright 1916 by Holt, Rinehart & Winston and renewed 1944 by Carl Sandburg, by permission of Harcourt Brace & Company.

Siegfried Sassoon: "Lamentations," Copyright 1918, 1920 by E.P. Dutton, Copyright 1936, 1946, 1947, 1948 by Siegfried Sassoon, and "Everyone Sang," Copyright 1920 by E.P. Dutton, Copyright renewed 1948 by Siegfried Sassoon, both from *Collected Poems* (E.P. Dutton), by permission of Viking Penguin, a division of Penguin Books USA Inc, and George Sassoon.

Simonides: "Cenotaph at the Isthmos" translated by Peter Jay, from Peter Jay (ed): *The Greek Anthology* (Penguin Books, 1973), Copyright © Peter Jay, 1973, by permission of Penguin Books Ltd.

Ken Smith: "Essential Serbo-Croat" from *Tender to the Queen of Spain* (Bloodaxe Books, 1993), by permission of the publisher.

Anna Świrszczyńska: "Building the Barricade", translated by Magnus Jan Krynski and Robert Maguire, from Desmond Graham (ed.): *Poetry of the Second World War: An International Anthology* (Chatto & Windus, 1995).

David Vogel: "Don't Be Afraid" from *The Penguin Book of Hebrew Verse*, edited and translated by T. Carmi (Penguin Books, 1981), Copyright © T. Carmi, 1981, by permission of Penguin Books Ltd.

Arthur Waley: poem number 122 "How few ..." from *The Book of Songs* translated by Arthur Waley, Copyright © 1937 by Arthur Waley, by permission of Grove/Atlantic, Inc.

W.B. Yeats: "What Was Lost," Copyright 1940 by Georgie Yeats, copyright renewed © 1968 by Bertha Georgie Yeats, Michael Butler Yeats and Anne Yeats; "An Irish Airman Forsees his Death," Copyright © 1919 by Macmillan Publishing Company, renewed 1947 by Bertha Georgie Yeats; both from *The Collected Works of W.B. Yeats, Volume I: The Poems*, revised and edited by Richard E. Finneran, by permission of Scribner, a Division of Simon & Schuster and A.P. Watt Ltd on behalf of Michael Yeats.

Sa'di Yusuf: "Guns" from *Modern Poetry of the Arab World*, edited and translated by Abdullah al-Udhari, (Penguin Books, 1986) translation, Copyright © Abdullah al-Udhari, 1986, by permission of Penguin Books Ltd.

DATE DUE

NOV 28 2002		